How to kind

To all the children who are reading this book,
always remember:

We rise by lifting others

Carly was excited, a smile spread across her **face,**
When she announced, "Mom, Dad, tomorrow is the **race!**"

You see, Carly had been training, training to be the **best,**
The very best swimmer, better than all the **rest.**

Carly swam in the mornings, she even swam every **night**,
Carly swam and swam and SWAM, with all her **might**.

She swam pretty well, but her biggest **wish,**
Was to swim as naturally as a super-fast **fish.**

When Carly looked in the mirror, what did she **see?**
"I see that swimming is the very BEST part of **me!**"

"It's the thing I'm best at, it's my very best **skill,**
and when I win each race I get a big **thrill.**"

Carly made sure she ate a big healthy **breakfast,**
Because she needed energy and had no time for **rest.**

"Goodbye, Mom and Dad, bye-bye sweety **cat**,
When I get home, I'll give you a big happy **pat**...

Because I'll be a winner, you'll all **see**,
Because swimming is the very best part of **me**!"

Carly met up with all her friends at **school**,
Then they hopped onto the bus and rode to the **pool**.

She began to warm up her legs, arms and **spine,**
Then it was time to line up at the starting **line.**

She lowered her goggles, and wiggled her **toes,**
Then the whistle blew, ready, set **go!**

Carly was swimming ever-so-**fast**,
One thing was for sure, she'd never come in **last**.

But she spotted something in the water **ahead**,
Something black and bobbing - a furry little **head!**

When she got closer that's when she could **see**,
The wet and bumbling and **drowning...**

"Bee! My gosh, aw, the poor little **thing,**
Its wings are all wet, it's really **struggling!"**

But her friends were all speeding right past **her,**
If she stopped swimming now, they would all beat **her.**

Carly couldn't bear to lose this **race**,
After all her bragging, how could she show her **face**?

For a horrible moment, she didn't know what to **do**,
What do you think you would do, if it was **you**?

But the moment passed very **quickly**,
The little bee looking more and more **sickly**.

"Oh, swimming is the best part of **me**,
But I must help set this little bee **free!**"

Carly took off her cap, scooped the bee **inside**,
Then carefully swam over to the **side**.

She didn't even know who had **won**,
As she gently placed the bee in the **sun**...

But it didn't really matter, Carly **thought**,
Thinking of the battle, the bee just **fought**.

She no longer felt that she had **lost**,
Saving a life was what mattered the **most**.

It gave her the very best feeling **inside**,
One that her big grin, just couldn't **hide**.

And even better than winning any **races,**
Was when she saw all the other smiling **faces.**

Her mum and dad, gave a wave and a **cheer,**
Carly waved back, grinning from ear to **ear.**

She couldn't wait, to see her **sweety-cat**,
And give her the promised happy **pat**.

"Hooray, hooray, for wonderful **Carly**!
She's a hero for stopping to save the **bee**!"

"That's when I knew kindness and **empathy**,
Are actually the very best parts of **me**!"

Printed in Great Britain
by Amazon